A
NIGHTMARE

LOST IN A FADED MEMORY

GAYATHRI REDDY YELLAMULA

Copyright © Gayathri Reddy Yellamula
All Rights Reserved.

ISBN 979-888606237-3

This book has been published with all efforts taken to make the material error-free after the consent of the author. However, the author and the publisher do not assume and hereby disclaim any liability to any party for any loss, damage, or disruption caused by errors or omissions, whether such errors or omissions result from negligence, accident, or any other cause.

While every effort has been made to avoid any mistake or omission, this publication is being sold on the condition and understanding that neither the author nor the publishers or printers would be liable in any manner to any person by reason of any mistake or omission in this publication or for any action taken or omitted to be taken or advice rendered or accepted on the basis of this work. For any defect in printing or binding the publishers will be liable only to replace the defective copy by another copy of this work then available.

ABOUT THE BOOK

NIGHTMARE, IS A BOOK DEDICATED TO MY
PAST ,

THIS IS NOT ONLY A BOOK BUT A REAL *&* AN
EMOTIONAL JOURNEY. COMPILED BY
GAYATHRI REDDY YELLAMULA."

Contents

ABOUT THE COMPILER & EDITOR OF THE BOOK

GAYATHRI REDDY YELLAMULA

THIS IS GAYATHRI REDDY YELLAMULA ,FROM NALGONDA,TELANGANA. A WRITER, TEACHER, BELIEVES IN ALMIGHTY. SAMYUKTHAM IS TAUGHT TO BE MY PEN NAME .FOND OF WRITING AS IT IS THERAPUTIC. CHILDISH THAN TO BE CRUEL AS AN ADULT. BELIEVED IN FREEDOM OF LOVE AND FREEDOM TO LIVE .CO-AUTHOR OF ECHOS FOR PAST, RAINDROPS,VIRAGO WARRIORS, LOST POETRY PAGES, AND BEING PUBLISHED IN ANTHOLOGY OF POETRY WORLD ORG . CAN BE SEARCHED IN INSTA @SAMYUKTHAM_7939, GAYATRIE_REDDY.

Preface

NIGHTMARE...

Nuevo
" A FADED MEMORY & THE LOST HOPE "

These are the most hardest days in my life,
Everything I have been loosing since many years.

This would be boring to read though, and for me, breaking into million pieces to recall that I've been facing hardest levels in the battle of life.

I felt , my blood would be my LAST HOPE, I've lost.

I was diving into the ocean of tears I once felt, but no I was deep inside the ocean ,I was lost in a fading memory with many broken dreams...

THAT DAY, had dinner the same way I used to , nothing gave me sign , no symptom had warned me through. Infact I was happy that afternoon as I was felt my twin baby's movements inside my tummy, I was happy, feeling that they will be kicking inside as they were feeling hungry, Sometimes I feel they were listening to my words and responding as well. I was overwhelmed many a time looking my tummy with my little ones. Soon this period of waiting completes , they would see their mom and dad's love towards them I wished...

AND THAT WAS THE WORST NIGHT EVER, around 12'o clock in the mid night, started feeling uneasy . Not able to breath completely. My lower abdomen started feeling light contractions. I was frightened, which made my heart beat faster and pushed my body into fight-and-flight mode. I felt I was sweating. Lost my confidence and rushed towards towards granny's home. She was concluded that they may be labor pains and immediately I had thought of calling my doctor, not knowing that I lost her contact . my hands started shivering while I was searching my brother in law's contact where I can surely get help from.

HE, the one who turned invisible to visible, he immediately taken doctor on line and SHE , the one who responded quickly and sent the ambulance to my place as a part of humanity . BUT,

As I have the cervical incompetence where I had a cercalage in 20th week of high risk pregnancy As my pelvic floor weakened with the vomitings in the entire period of pregnancy, with the increased growth of kids inside tummy , must realize the thing that this was really high in risk to protect twin kids than that of singleton..

My fate, AMBULANCE had arrived. Besides that twin A Water broke. By having the contractions for every half a minute my baby pushing the way with pressure. Membranes ruptured . I know babies born after such an early water break are less likely to live. Im tensed screaming with pains,,.

After getting into the ambulance my twin A's little leg has come out ,I was screaming, shouting, as my entire body started aching , it was like my backbone was breaking into some million pieces,.. near to death it was.

Near to the hospital , another ones water had also broke. I was getting unconscious with that heart breaking situation. Mentally it was like paralyzing .Rushed immediately into hospital where the process of labor started and the pains were more ,

was screamed initially to hide roars within, lied down in an excrutiatingly uncomfortable position, contractions were more with abruptly gradual moments of fetus, scratching bed with unendurable cramps,eyes were bled dried tears at every pull. Heartbeat ran stoppingly when my nerves twitched and pinched, had reaching the doors of death,,,

I was given birth to baby boy first. After 10 minutes for a baby girl too...

My first baby left me after sometime the same time I was listening to my daughter's first cry...I hoped atleast she was safe, but I listened , doctor was saying to hope less than 1% . I was broken into pieces many pieces where I never wanted to live anymore .. how can I answer to my husband now, what was my mistake, I was in a shock , how would I show my face to him. I didn't wanna live anymore I would have died instead of my kid...

Baby was put in incubator for 2 days , My husband was immediately arrived after knowing , I couldn't imagine his pain for losing his kids and looking me in that situation ,

He saw his daughter who would be his love,

who would deserve his love the most,

who would be the only one to hold his happiness in his life,

FOUGHT for her a lot , we knew we were financially had no support anywhere, but He said , he would not let our baby to go for this reason anymore. But hopelessly, our baby didn't wanna leave his brother alone in the heaven ,, she left us and made us alone again...

I felt this chapter was ended here, NO...no.. this made me realize very hardly , that my kids came for a reason to make me more stronger than IAM...!

THEY MADE ME REALISE, whom to love, however the situations changed...everyone started blaming me, started criticizing me , forgot their love and affection which was shown earlier finally.

" I SUFFERED NAUSEA THROUGHOUT THE TERM , I SUFFERED FOR NOT ABLE TO BREATH, I SUFFERED WITH VOMITINGS FOR 5 TO 8 TIMES PER A DAY, I SUFFERED MANY SLEEPLESS NIGHTS, I SUFFERED WITH BACKACHE , I SUFFERED FOR NOT GETTING ENOUGH LOVE OR AFFECTION FROM MANY, IN THIS PERIOD OF TIME, I WAS MILES AWAY FROM THE PERSON WHOM I LOVE THE MOST, I WAS VERY HOPEFULL THAT IAM GOING TO SEE MY HOPE, I CARRIED FOR 26 WEEKS, I LOST,,, I LOST..."

HOWEVER , people changed, situations changed, myself lost in the depth of ocean of tears..!

I was broken and hurting. Iam not being able to accept this news. Many conflicting emotions pulling me down .

Sickness plagued me and my depression. First thing i realised is life is a rollercoaster., we dont realise what we have untill it is gone. Once we accept something painful, life changes.

On that next day when i was waiting to see my child, i could think nothing but predict . The closer I reach my heart thumped with great vigour, I still waited for a mirracle until the last second I have seen her. I still couldnt find the key to emancipation to unlock the bondage.

May be the wounds of internal walls of my weakened body heal ,but scars on my mental abortive stage would no be concealed soon .

It hurts , that I failed , placing my trembling hands on my belly where I hoped to convey my unspoken words of assurance and promises to my kids. Being the only one to know from days within the womb, I haven't saved. It's unfair, It is a process of emotions, but accepting reality is the only way to live in present.

-GAYATHRI REDDY YELLAMULA.

PREFACE

ΦΦΦ

Acknowledgements

THANKYOU...

Nuevo

IT TOOK SOME TWELVE YEARS AND THREE DRAFTS TO STEP FOREWARD TO REACH YOU WITH A BOOK ,BUT WITH A HOPEFUL CONTENT . IT WAS TRUE, IN THE BEGINNING WE WERE JUST A WRITER , A PEN , PAPER , BUT AT THE END IT SHAPED ME ALOT AND MADE AN EMOTIONAL CONTENT WHICH WAS FINISHED READING BY YOU..

Prologue

THE PROBLEM WITH CONSTANTLY HOPING ON SOMETHING TO HAPPEN WOULD BE LIKE "THE TASTE OF HOPE FADES AWAY AND WE SHOULD NOT CARE ANYMORE" BECAUSE IT IS OUR PAIN AND REALITY TOO.

ᗛᗛᗛ

www.ingramcontent.com/pod-product-compliance
Lightning Source LLC
Chambersburg PA
CBHW020858160726

47993CB00004B/1720